Time Pieces for Treble/Alto Recorder

VOLUME 1

Arranged by Kathryn Bennetts & Peter Bowman

ABRSM
Printed on materials from sustainable sources

CONTENTS

Sakura, Sakura

Trad. (Japanese)

arr. Alan Bullard

Sakura Cherry Blossom

AB 2845

Kalevala Melody

Trad. (Finnish)
arr. Alan Bullard

The Nutting Girl

Trad. (English)
arr. Alan Bullard

c.1340 Douce dame jolie

(Virelai)

Guillaume de Machaut

(c.1300–1377)

arr. Alan Bullard

A 'virelai' is a medieval French lyric poem.

AB 2845

c.1530 La rocha el fuso
(Galliard)

Anon.
arr. Alan Bullard

A 'galliard' is a lively dance, generally in triple time.

c.1610 La volta

from Fitzwilliam Virginal Book

William Byrd
(*c.*1540–1623)
arr. Alan Bullard

This is a lively dance (from Italian *voltare*, 'to turn').

c.1670   Minuet

Jean-Baptiste Lully
(1632–1687)
arr. Alan Bullard

*c.*1690 Prelude

from *Te Deum*, H. 146

Marc-Antoine Charpentier
(1643–1704)

1762 Allegro
K. 3

Wolfgang Amadeus Mozart
(1756–1791)

AB 2845

1787 The Ploughboy
from *The Farmer*

William Shield
(1748–1829)

arr. Alan Bullard

Fine

D.S. al Fine

AB 2845

1797 Poco adagio

from String Quartet Op. 76 No. 3 ('Emperor')

Joseph Haydn
(1732–1809)

1823 Entr'acte
from *Rosamunde*

Franz Schubert
(1797–1828)

1848 Melody

from *Album for the Young*, Op. 68 No. 1

Robert Schumann
(1810–1856)

arr. Alan Bullard

1875 **Solveig's Song**

from *Peer Gynt*

Edvard Grieg
(1843–1907)

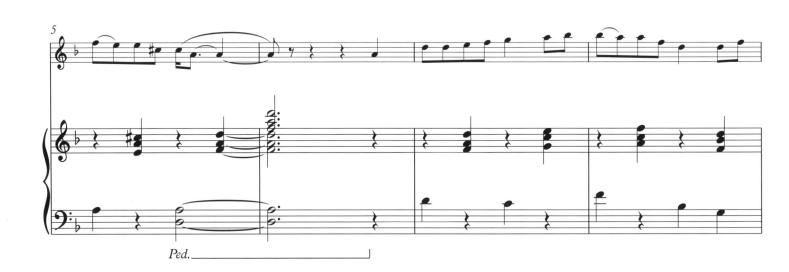

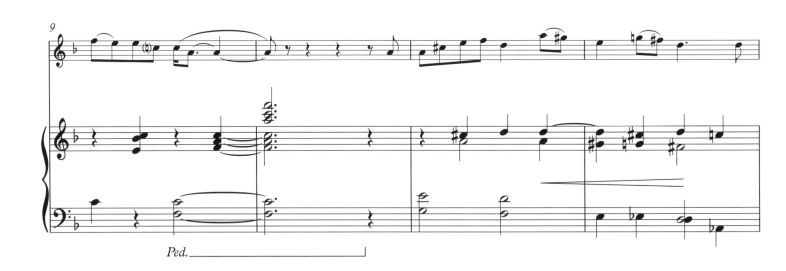

1888 Theme from Symphony No. 1

(Third Movement)

Gustav Mahler
(1860–1911)

AB 2845

1896 To a Wild Rose

from *Woodland Sketches*

Edward MacDowell
(1860–1908)

AB 2845

1926 Muskrat Ramble

Kid Ory (1886–1973)

arr. Alan Bullard

1935 Fishing Song

from *Friday Afternoons*, Op. 7

Benjamin Britten
(1913–1976)

AB 2845

1946 Sorrow

from *For Children*, Vol. 2

Béla Bartók
(1881–1945)

Time Pieces for Treble/Alto Recorder

VOLUME 1

Arranged by Kathryn Bennetts & Peter Bowman

ABRSM
Printed on materials from sustainable sources

Sakura, Sakura

Trad. (Japanese)
arr. Alan Bullard

Sakura   Cherry Blossom

Kalevala Melody

Trad. (Finnish)
arr. Alan Bullard

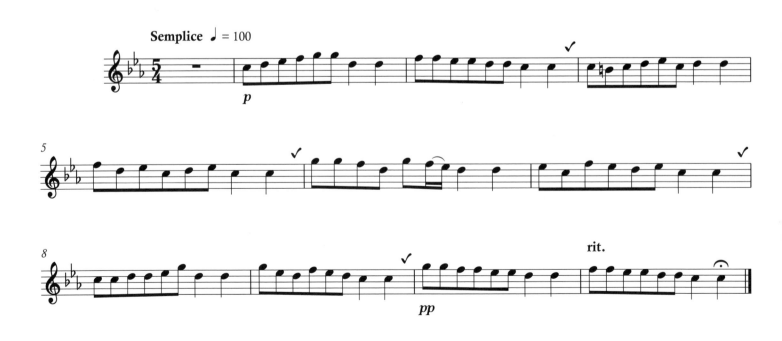

AB 2845

The Nutting Girl

Trad. (English)
arr. Alan Bullard

*c.*1340   Douce dame jolie
(Virelai)

Guillaume de Machaut
(*c.*1300–1377)
arr. Alan Bullard

A 'virelai' is a medieval French lyric poem.

La rocha el fuso
(Galliard)

Anon.
arr. Alan Bullard

A 'galliard' is a lively dance, generally in triple time.

c.1610

La volta
from Fitzwilliam Virginal Book

William Byrd
(c.1540–1623)
arr. Alan Bullard

This is a lively dance (from Italian *voltare*, 'to turn').

AB 2845

c.1670 Minuet

Jean-Baptiste Lully
(1632–1687)
arr. Alan Bullard

c.1690 Prelude
from *Te Deum*, H. 146

Marc-Antoine Charpentier
(1643–1704)

1762 Allegro
K. 3

Wolfgang Amadeus Mozart
(1756–1791)

1787 The Ploughboy
from *The Farmer*

William Shield
(1748–1829)
arr. Alan Bullard

AB 2845

1797 Poco adagio
from String Quartet Op. 76 No. 3 ('Emperor')

Joseph Haydn
(1732–1809)

1823 Entr'acte
from *Rosamunde*

Franz Schubert
(1797–1828)

1848 Melody
from *Album for the Young*, Op. 68 No. 1

Robert Schumann
(1810–1856)

arr. Alan Bullard

1875 Solveig's Song
from *Peer Gynt*

Edvard Grieg
(1843–1907)

1888 Theme from Symphony No. 1
(Third Movement)

Gustav Mahler
(1860–1911)

1896 To a Wild Rose
from *Woodland Sketches*

Edward MacDowell
(1860–1908)

1926 Muskrat Ramble

Kid Ory (1886–1973)

arr. Alan Bullard

1935 Fishing Song
from *Friday Afternoons*, Op. 7

Benjamin Britten
(1913–1976)

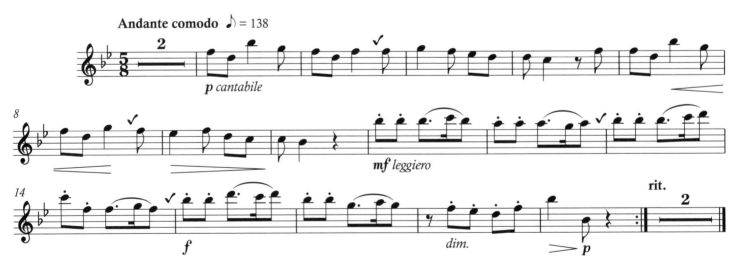

1946 Sorrow

from *For Children*, Vol. 2

Béla Bartók
(1881–1945)

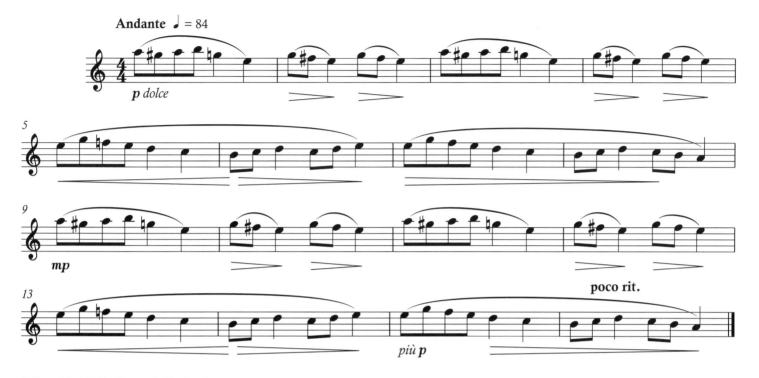

2006 Chalk and Cheese

Kathryn Bennetts
(b. 1956)

2006   Fancy

Kathryn Bennetts
(b. 1956)

2006   Colourful G

Kathryn Bennetts
(b. 1956)

Music origination by
Barnes Music Engraving Ltd, East Sussex

Printed in England by Caligraving Ltd, Thetford, Norfolk